Dedicated to my children

Noelle, Courtney and Jonathan

The n's Justify the Means

Cover design by John A. Mosier Jr.

Book design by John A. Mosier Jr.

Library of Congress

TX-0007180040 2010 1-313799741 2010
ISBN: 978-0-557-19678-4

Printed in the United States of America

First Printing: January 2010

John A. Mosier Jr.

Currently the co-founder, President & CEO of Transblock Corporation, Mr. Mosier has served over 21 years as a Quality Management professional. Twelve of which were spent with the General Motors Corporation as a Senior Supplier Quality/Development Engineer. During that period of time Mr. Mosier effectively coached and applied these simple methodologies to various locations globally, which included:

- General Motors Corporation -North American Vehicle Operations
- General Motors Corporation –Latin America
- General Motors Corporation –Europe
- General Motors Corporation –Asia Pacific

He has earned a Bachelors of Science & Engineering Degree in Quality Control & Quality Assurance from Kennedy-Western University.

Official publications include "Application of Robust Design Methods to 2002 Chevrolet Avalanche Sail Panel", published in U.S. and Japan (JSQE) in 04/02, personally requested and presided over by Dr. Genichi Taguchi.

In addition to co-authoring a patent for the world's first ground transient elimination filter, he has also consulted to some major organizations which include Caterpillar Corporation, Harley Davidson and Lockheed Martin.

4

"Quality is never an accident; it is always the result of high intention, sincere effort, intelligent direction and skillful execution; it represents the wise choice of many alternatives".

William A. Foster

"The bitterness of poor quality is remembered long after the sweetness of low price has faded from memory"

Aldo Gucci

"When you're out of quality, you're out of business".

Unknown

Introduction

A case study approach was used in this study to examine a manufacturing process that could be prone to poor quality. This manufacturing organization does not have a method in place to track costs associated with product failure. The manufacturing process that was selected for this study was the seat belt retractor sensor assembly. The process used for this part is both labor-intensive and error prone. The components used in this process include purchased parts and manufactured parts. The parts are not inspected during the assembly process, but are tested at the end of the process. Each part that fails requires reworking, which is both time consuming and expensive. The company producing the part can invoice the purchasing organization $17.00 for each part. Included in this cost is the per unit profit. While the company cannot bill additionally for units that required reworking, each reworked unit costs the company $3.10 in profits.

The costs of initiating new procedures to reduce failures included implementing a vision system to check parts at each step in the process. The costs associated with this system were approximately $25,000. Using the formula presented in the review of literature, the return on investment was $364.25, which indicated a substantial improvement in net profit could be realized if the producing company implemented this capital equipment to reduce failure and improve quality.

The purpose of this study was to develop a comprehensive approach to successful implementing a formal "Cost of Quality" program in an organization that could be used to track costs associated with both good and poor quality. The study regarding costs associated with poor quality is important because controlling these costs can have a positive effect on the net profit of a company.

List of Tables

List of Figures

Chapter 1 – Importance of the Study

Much has been said in the newspapers, radio, television, conversations, everywhere - about the need for reduction in waste and rework, and improvement in productivity and quality. Global competition makes quality more than a "nice thing to have" and has become essential for survival (Ragsdell, 2001). Many organizations - business and government alike - have started using quality tools, building teams, and looking for quality improvement opportunities. The most important opportunities for improvement lie in two frequently untouched areas: analysis of the flow, or process, of one's work today, and a concept called the *Cost of Quality*, which is the topic of this paper.

Most companies relate the term "quality" to their products or services Quality exceeds this narrow scope. Processes, and even systems, can also meet objectives or expectations. When an organization applies the quality concept to its processes and its entire management system, it can begin to see an effect on its bottom line.

The true cost of quality is often lost across vertical and horizontal business functions within most organizations. A cost of quality approach examines processes and events in both a preventative and corrective environment and derives a cost that can be analyzed in the context of the business cycle (Quartararo, 1999). The objective of a cost of quality process is to capture the total value of poor quality in an organization and provide a vehicle that justifies the elimination of poor quality.

Companies also wishing (sometimes required to) obtain ISO-9000 or TS-16949 certification can find that ISO-9000 requirements necessitates the need and proper adherence to "Cost of Quality" principles (Ragsdell, 2002).

State the Problem

Major quality disconnects, such as increasing customer expectations, global competition, and mergers and acquisitions, challenge the ability of companies to sustain sales growth and profitability during times of economic turndown (Beecroft, 1999). Unfortunately, some organizations respond with a slash-and-burn approach to cost reduction, eliminating productive, as well as nonproductive, activities. The key to achieving effective cost reduction is to correctly measure the real business failure costs associated with quality disconnects. Quantification of failure cost, followed by rigorous implementation of actions to eliminate their causes can lead to cost reductions amounting to 10%, while experiencing a similarly significant increase in customer satisfaction.

In the battle for global market share, the company that creates customer confidence with on time delivery of defect-free, reliable products and services is the company that can be expected to succeed (Creveling, 2000). Customer satisfaction cannot be a frill or a fluke; it is an imperative for companies wishing to earn or maintain world class stature. Quality is the gateway to American business success in the global free-for-all for customer satisfaction and loyalty. If organizations are to seize the phenomenal growth opportunities on the horizon, they must clarify their quality goals and quantify the means to attain them.

Quality-related activities can range from 25% to 60% of the total production costs of a company. Determining the value of these activities by using quality cost techniques quantifies both the value-added and non-value-added costs of a quality system. This analysis lends itself to the use of quality cost techniques as a management tool for guiding the continuous improvement efforts of a company.

The fundamental quality cost improvement strategy is to attack failure costs and drive them to zero. This strategy can be accomplished only by problem solving and improving processes that produce the product or service. This book demonstrates a systematic approach/methodology to establishing, implementing and maintaining a formal Cost of Quality program that can be utilized in the business world today.

Purpose of the Book

The quality-related costs were much larger than had been shown in the accounting reports. For companies these costs ran in the range of 20 to 40% of sales (Juran, 1979).The quality costs were not simply the result of factory operation; the support operations were also major contributors. The bulk of costs were the result of poor quality. Such costs are often included in the standards, but they were in fact avoidable. While costs associated with poor quality were avoidable, no clear responsibility was determined for action to reduce them. Neither was there any structured approach for doing so. These findings emerged slowly, amid a good deal of confusion. At the outset many quality specialists took their companies into vague quality cost "programs" without being clear on the objectives (Juran, 1979). Gradually the objectives emerged in two main forms:

1. Estimate the costs of poor quality as a "one-shot" study, and then use the findings to identify specific projects for improvement

2. Expand the accounting system to quantify quality costs, and then publish the results as a continuing scoreboard. The expectation was that the published figures would stimulate managers to take action to reduce the costs.

These two objectives are interrelated. Some companies, which opted for objective 1, used the estimates to identify improvement projects, after which they actually made improvements. Having done so, they found that to hold the gains they needed controls, including financial controls. Those financial controls were then established based on quantifying the pertinent quality costs. While there is logic behind both objectives 1 and 2, getting actual cost reductions solely through publication has turned out to be illusory. By themselves, the published figures do not stimulate action unless the company sets up a structured process for quality improvement. Identifying specific products is a necessary step in the structured approach, but it is not sufficient. The full structure must be set up.

Statement of the Problem

The objective of the present study is to develop a comprehensive approach to successful implementation of a formal "Cost of Quality" program in an organization that can be used to track costs associated with both good and poor quality.

The following Items were addressed in the following study:

- Categories of Poor Quality

- Return on Investment (ROI)

- Controversial Cost Categories

- Making the Initial Cost Study

- Presentation of Initial Findings to Management

- Gaining Approval for the Quality Improvement Program

- Discovering the Optimum

- Scoreboard on the Cost of Poor Quality

- Why Cost of Quality Programs Fail

- Roadmap for Introducing a System for Reporting the Cost of Poor Quality

Importance of the Study

This study is needed to present supporting data that the cost of poor quality can substantially impact the profit that a manufacturing company makes. By understanding how these costs can be controlled from the beginning of the manufacturing process instead of trying to compensate for them as throughout the process, engineers and managers can contribute to the success of the organization.

Scope of the Study

The final paper provided a detailed approach to implementing a sound Cost of Quality program that can provide the basis of information which any manufacturing company may employ to optimize costs. The steps needed to implement this type of program are presented in a generalized manner to allow their adaptation by both large and small organizations.

Rationale of the Study

Many manufacturing organizations are unaware of the total effect that "Cost of Poor Quality" has on the bottom line of their company. Without this knowledge, profits can be lost. For example, a company that was producing $20 million dollars a year in profits was asked if they formally tracked scrap costs within their organization. Management indicated that the expense associated with tracking this type of activity on parts with minimal values could be a waste of time (Chase,

1999). Further analysis showed that scrap, and their related costs, amounted to 5% of their total throughput, and costs of poor quality were exceeding $1 million a year. Many companies fail to see the need to have the capacity to plan, design, track, and maintain assets in real-time, while eliminating waste and providing a higher return on investment. These reasons support the need to analyze the cost of quality, or more precisely, the cost of poor quality, and develop a method to track these expenses as a means of controlling them in the future.

Definition of Terms

Cost of poor quality (COPQ): Costs associated with providing poor quality products or services. According to (Knackstedt, 2003), four categories of costs have been delineated: a) internal failure costs (costs associated with defects found before the customer receives the product or service); b) external failure costs (costs associated with defects found after the customer receives the product or service); c) appraisal costs (costs incurred to determine the degree of conformance to quality requirements) and d) prevention costs (costs incurred to keep failure and appraisal costs to a minimum).

Cost of quality (COQ): A term used by Crosby (Knackstedt, 2003) referring to the cost of poor quality.

Quality: A subjective term for which each person has his or her own definition (Knackstedt, 2003). In technical usage, quality can have two meanings: a) the characteristics of a product or service that bear on its ability to satisfy stated or implied needs; and b) a product or service free of deficiencies.

Quality circles: Quality improvement or self-improvement study groups composed of a small number of employees (10 or fewer) and their supervisor (Knackstedt, 2003). Quality circles originated in Japan, where they are called quality control circles.

Quality engineering: The analysis of a manufacturing system at all stages to maximize the quality of the process itself and the products it produces (Knackstedt, 2003).

Quality loss function: A parabolic approximation of the quality loss that occurs when a quality characteristic deviates from its target value (Knackstedt, 2003). The quality loss function is expressed in monetary units: the cost of deviating from the target increases quadratically the further the quality characteristic moves from the target. The formula used to compute the quality loss function depends on the type of quality characteristic being used. The quality loss function was first introduced in this form by Genichi Taguchi.

Quality management (QM): The application of a quality management system in managing a process to achieve maximum customer satisfaction at the lowest overall cost to the organization while continuing to improve the process (Knackstedt, 2003).

Total quality: A strategic integrated system for achieving customer satisfaction that involves all managers and employees and uses quantitative methods to continuously improve an organization's processes (Knackstedt, 2003).

Overview of the Study

This study details a systematic approach of how to implement a formal Cost of Quality program within an organization. The study demonstrates cost advantages as a result of such implementation of this type of system by revealing numerous categories of waste that often exceed the scope of most traditional accounting systems. The study outlines a generalized methodology that provides support for the conjecture that quality does not cost more – quality saves money. Quality management programs, properly planned and implemented, have been shown to reduce operating costs (Beecroft, 1999).

Cost of quality (CoQ) is an accounting technique introduced by Juran in 1951 to provide justification to management for investments in process improvements (Hagan, 1986), or as Crosby (1979) has promoted the concept, "to get management's attention and to provide a measurement base for seeing how quality improvement is doing." However, the use of CoQ has been expanded beyond its initial purpose of demonstrating return on investment of quality efforts. It has been widely used in manufacturing and service industries both for controlling the costs of quality activities and for identifying opportunities to reduce quality costs.

The basis for CoQ is the accounting of two kinds of costs: those which are incurred due to a lack of quality and those which are incurred in the achievement of quality (Houston, 2001). Costs due a lack of quality are further divided into costs of internal failures and costs of external failures. Costs of achieving quality are further divided into appraisal cost and defect prevention costs. Figure 1 illustrates this breakdown.

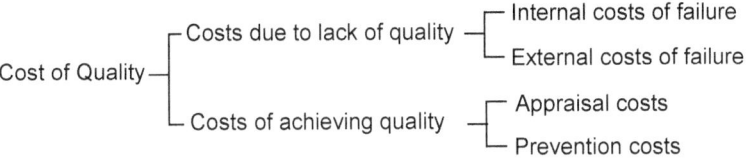

Figure 1 - Breakdown of Cost of Quality

Chapter 2 - Review of Related Literature

Review of Related Literature

All organizations make use of the concept of identifying the costs needed to carry out the various functions—product development, marketing, personnel, production, etc. Until the 1950s, this concept had not been extended to the quality function, except for the departmental activities of inspection and test (Juran, 1979). Many other quality-related costs have been determined, but they were scattered among various accounts, especially "overhead" accounts. During the 1950s, numerous quality-oriented staff departments evolved in large organizations. The heads of these new departments were faced with "selling" their activities to company managers. Because the main language of those managers was money, the concept of studying quality-related costs emerged as a means of communication between the quality staff departments and the company managers.

Categories of Poor Quality

Cost of Poor Quality allows a company to track things that have already manifested themselves as problems (Chase, 1999). Companies that wish to become proactive need a more inclusive cost of quality system. Separating quality expenses into four categories, internal failures, external failures, appraisal and prevention, appears to be an effective method (Houston & Keats, 2001). Table 1 defines the four categories and indicates typical costs associated with each category.

Table 1 - Definition of Cost of Quality Categories

Category	Definition	Typical Costs for Software
Internal failures	Quality failures detected prior to product shipment	Defect management, rework, retesting
External failures	Quality failures detected after product shipment	Technical support, complaint investigation, defect notification
Appraisal	Discovering the condition of the product	Testing and associated activities, product quality audits
Prevention	Efforts to ensure product quality	Supplier quality assurance (SQA) administration, inspections, process improvements, metrics collection and analysis

Note: Houston & Keats, 2001, p. 1.

Combining a cost of poor quality and the four costs of quality categories together can put the individuals back in control of the quality system, by shifting from a reaction-based system to one that is proactive in controlling quality.

Controversial Cost Categories

As detailed categories of the cost of poor quality are identified, some may be considered controversial. Much of the controversy centers around the point that these costs are not related to quality, but are costs that are included in normal operating expenses. Therefore, these costs should not be included (Juran, 1979). Examples of these types of costs include:

1. Inclusion of overhead on top of direct labor and direct material costs of scrap and rework (i.e., one approach is to include variable overhead but exclude fixed overhead costs.)

2. Unavoidable manufacturing waste. These parts are not defective, but trim removed from the beginning of a coil of wire, excess material surrounding a molded plastic part, spillage of a chemical loaded into a process. It is argued that this is a normal part of operating a process.

3. Profit lost on scrapped product.

4. Product liability costs.

5. Depreciation on measuring equipment.

6. Preventive maintenance. (Many controversial categories are classified as prevention costs. Ironically, prevention usually accounts for less than 5% of the total quality cost.)

7. Tool maintenance.

8. Loss in morale.

9. Production delays due to a high scrap rate.

10. Loss in customer good will and sales (Juran, 1979).

Arguments about the inclusion of such categories in determining the cost of poor quality can result in the downfall of the entire study. If numbers are included in the analysis without prior agreement, then doubt is cast on the entire study because it is claimed that the controversial costs were included to increase the total.

In many companies, the cost of poor quality is a large sum, and may be larger than the company's profits (Juran, 1979). As this cost analysis is true even when controversial categories are not included, it may be prudent to omit these categories as a means of avoiding controversy and focusing attention on major areas of potential cost reduction. Generally, efforts to quantify costs of quality have failed because of the insistence by some specialists that certain controversial categories be included or excluded.

A useful guide is to ask: "Suppose all defects disappeared. Would the cost in question also disappear?" A "yes" answer means that the cost is associated with quality problems and therefore should be included in the report. A "no" answer means that the category should not be included in the cost of poor quality. At a minimum, controversial categories should be separated out of the totals to focus attention toward the main issues.

Another controversy concerns categorization of cost items. Some examples of these controversies include:

1. Should 100% of inspection costs be included as part of appraisal costs or internal failure costs? If the 100% inspection was performed to improve an unsatisfactory quality level, then it is part of an internal failure cost. If the quality level is satisfactory but 100% inspection is performed because of a requirement by the customer, then the cost is an appraisal cost.

2. Should costs of investigating and correcting causes of failures be included as part of prevention costs for poor quality? The point is made that investigations can prevent future defects. If investigations were initiated because of actual failures, than such efforts should be included as failure costs. Design reviews and other activities connected with the evaluation of new designs should be classified as prevention. Such controversies should be settled quickly (even if arbitrarily) and not permitted to divert attention from the main target – failure costs.

3. Should costs that are also incurred but may result in understating the costs of poor quality be included? These "hidden" costs may include:

   a. Potential lost sales.

   b. Costs of redesign due to quality reasons.

4. Costs of changing manufacturing processes due to inability to meet quality requirements.

5. Costs of software changes due to quality reasons.

6. Costs included in standards because history shows that a certain level of defects is inevitable and allowances should be included in standards:

   a. *Extra material purchased*: The purchasing agent orders 5% more than the production quantity needed.

   b. *Allowances for scrap and rework during production*: History shows that 3% is "normal" and accountants have built this amount into the cost standards. One accountant said, "Our scrap cost is zero. We make about 3% defective and have built this into our standard cost system. The production departments are able to stay within this 3% and therefore the scrap cost is zero."

   c. *Allowances in time standards for scrap and rework*: One manufacturer allows 9.6% in the time standard for certain operations to cover scrap and rework.

In such cases, management becomes concerned only when the standard value is exceeded. However, even when operating within those standards, the costs should be considered to be a part of the cost of poor quality. They represent opportunities for improvement.

1. Extra manufacturing costs due to defects, including additional costs for space, inventory charges, and overtime.

2. Scrap not reported, meaning scrap that is never reported because of fear of reprisals, or scrap that is charged to a general ledger account without an identification as scrap.

3. Excess process costs for acceptable product. For example, a process for filling packages with a dry soap mix meets requirements for label weight on the contents. However, the process aim is set above label weight to account for the variability in the filling process. If the variability is "large" then the aim must be set far enough above the minimum to accommodate the variability. A reduction in variability could mean setting the aim closer to the minimum, reducing the average amount of overfill.

4. Cost of errors made in support operations (e.g., order filling, production control, etc.).

5. Costs of poor quality are made within a supplier's plant, with these costs are included in the selling price.

These hidden costs can accumulate, affecting profit. Kane (1978) reported a potential multiplier effect of 3 or 4 times the reported failure cost. These costs should be included in the initial study on the cost of poor quality if agreement can be reached to include some of these costs and credible data or estimates are available. Table 2 presents an example of these costs.

Table 2 - Annual Quality Cost - Tire Manufacturer

1. Cost of quality failures –losses	Estimated Cost	Percentage
a. Defective stock	$ 3,276	0.37
b. Repairs to product	$ 73,229	8.31
c. Collect scrap	$ 2,288	0.26
d. Waste-scrap	$187,428	21.26
e. Consumer adjustments	$408,200	46.31
f. Downgrading products	$ 22,838	2.59
g Customer ill will	Not counted	
h. Customer police adj.	Not counted	
Total	$697,259	79.10%
2. Cost of appraisal		
a. Incoming inspection	$ 32,655	2.68
b. Inspection 1	$ 32.582	3.70
c. Inspection 2	$ 25,200	2.86
d. Spot-check inspection	$ 65.910	7.37
Total	$147,347	16.61%
3. Cost of prevention		
a. Local plant Quality control engineering	$ 7,848	0.89
b. Corporate Quality engineering	$ 30,000	3.40
Total	$ 37,848	4.29%
Grand total	$882,454	100.00%

Discovering the Optimum

When cost summaries on quality are first presented to managers, one usual question is: "What are the right costs?" The managers are looking for a standard ("par") against which to compare their actual costs so that they can make a judgment on whether there is a need for action.

Unfortunately few credible data are available. Companies almost never publish such data. Attempts to conduct research on these costs have encountered several obstacles:

1. Cost data are confidential and most companies do not release the information.

2. Definitions of quality costs vary by company. For example, some companies include unavoidable manufacturing waste as a part of the cost of poor quality while other companies do not; some companies add overhead to the direct cost of labor and material on scrap and rework, while other companies do not.

Wide ranges in published examples are a reminder of the risk in comparing quality costs in one company with industry averages. According to Juran (1979), three conclusions stand out: a) the total costs are higher for complex industries, b) failure costs are the largest percent of the total, and c) prevention costs are a small percent of the total.

The costs of achieving quality and the costs due to lack of quality have an inverse relationship to one another: as investment in achieving quality increases, costs due to lack of quality decrease. This relationship and its effect on the total cost of quality (TCoQ) are normally shown as a set of two-dimensional curves which plot costs against a measure of quality. In traditional CoQ models, the TCoQ has a point of diminishing returns, a minimum prior to achieving 100% of the quality measure. (See Figure 2.)

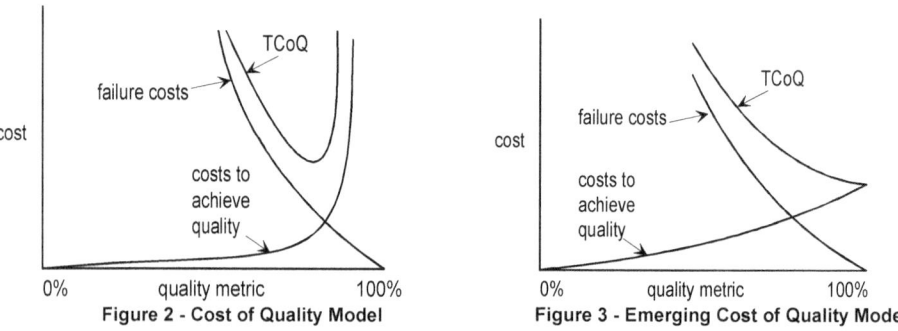

Figure 2 - Cost of Quality Model   **Figure 3 - Emerging Cost of Quality Model**

Note: Houston, 2001.

Manufacturing experience has shown that increased attention to defect prevention leads to large reductions in appraisal costs. This experience, reflected in the 1988 publication of "An Emerging Cost of Quality Model" (Gryna, 1988), extended the minimum TCoQ to 100%. (See Figure 3.) Although the latter model is an ideal that failed to acknowledge a law of diminishing returns, its premise that the optimum TCoQ could be shifted toward 100% suggested a dynamic CoQ model in which time was treated as a third dimension.

The dynamic dimension of the optimum cost of quality has been studied by Wasserman and Lindland (1996). Dynamism in CoQ models can be attributed to factors such as changing market pressures and perceptions of quality. Changing market pressures drive quality initiatives which, as Wasserman and Lindland indicated, can move the optimum to the right, in the direction of improvement. Conversely, as perceptions of quality in a product market mature and product quality remains constant, external failure costs can be expected to increase over time, shifting the optimum to the left.

34

Scoreboard on the Cost of Poor Quality

Some companies use periodic reporting on the cost of poor quality in the form of a scoreboard that can be put to certain constructive uses. However, creating and maintaining the scoreboard requires a considerable expenditure of time and effort. According to Gyrna, 1988, prior to undertaking such expenditure, the company should look beyond the assertions of the advocate and examine realities derived from experience. (Many companies have constructed quality cost scoreboards and have then abandoned them as not achieving the results promised by the advocates.) Whether or not to have such a scoreboard involves a number of issues, which are summarized in Table 3.

Table 3 - Quality Scoreboard Issues

Assertions	Realities
Publications of the cost figures can stimulate cost reductions.	Publications alone cannot result in cost reduction unless the company is well set up to identify projects, and organize for improvement.
Knowledge of these costs enable organizations to transfer charges to the guilty departments, thereby stimulating improvement.	True, provided a) the organization is aware of who is guilty and b) the company is well organized to identify and carry out improvement projects.
A financial scoreboard is needed for these costs just as the organization does for any other kinds of costs.	A valid reason, but the choice of standards is important. Standards for these costs should be the level reached after a quality improvement program has decreased costs. Otherwise cost controls can help perpetuate the high level of costs.
A financial scoreboard is needed to help hold gains resulting from the quality improvement program.	Usually correct, of course, such a scoreboard is created after the costs have been reduced. In this way, control is applied to the improved level.
The figures are needed to identify similar projects that cannot be identified through broad estimates.	A valid reason if the organization has already made some of the big gains.
The figure are needed for contract reasons, (e.g. to bid for business, or because a major client asks to see them).	These reasons are persuasive.
Conferences and published papers reported how other companies have gotten good results from quantifying these costs.	Seldom an adequate reason. Published reports are biased. (People do not report their failure stories).

Roadmap for Introducing a System for Reporting the Cost of Poor Quality

Results can have a striking impact on management if the presentation provides the magnitude of the total cost and identifies areas for improvement.

Use of the grand total to demonstrate need for quality improvement.

The most significant figure in a quality cost study is the total of the quality costs. The total may be so small as to fail to compete for managerial priority. For example, avoidable quality costs in a confectionery company totaled $44,500 per year. Managers decided that any program to reduce these costs would have to wait, since numerous other problems had higher priority.

More usually, managers are stunned by the size of the total costs – they had no idea the amount was so large. One example was a leading manufacturer of aircraft engines. When total quality costs were made known to the managing director, he promptly convened his senior executives to discuss a broad plan of action

Those presenting the report should be prepared to be greeted with skepticism. The costs associated with poor quality may be such that they may not be believed. This skepticism could be avoided if management has previously agreed to definitions of the cost categories and if the accounting function had either collected the data or had been associated with the data collection process.

Relating the grand total to business measures.

Interpretation of the total is aided by relating total quality costs to other figures with which managers are familiar. Relationships that have the greatest impact on upper management are:

- *Quality costs as a percent of sales*: Financial reports to upper managers and shareholders make extensive use of sales as bases for comparison. When quality costs are similarly related to sales, upper management is able to grasp the significance of the numbers more easily.

- *Quality costs compared to profit*: Managers are surprised to learn that quality costs may exceed the company's profit (which often they do.) A component manufacturer with a strong reputation for quality reported direct costs of scrap and rework of $7.5 million versus a profit of $1.5 million (Juran, 1979).

- *Quality costs compared to the magnitude of current problems*: While money is the universal language of upper management, additional ways are available to convey the importance of quality costs to these managers. Two universal languages are spoken in an organization. At the "bottom" the language is of things and deeds: square meters of floor space, schedules of 400 tons per week, rejection rates of 3.6%. At the "top" the language is money: sales, profit, taxes, investment.

One company that was preoccupied with meeting delivery schedules translated the quality costs into equivalent-added production. As this process coincided with chief goals of the managers, their interest was aroused. The total cost of quality was estimated to be equivalent to one of the company plants employing 2,900 people, occupying 1.1 million sq. ft. of space and requiring $6 million of in-process inventory. These latter three figures in turn meant the equivalent of one of their major plants making 100% defective work every working day of the year. What is ironic about this situation is that the company is the quality leader in its industry.

Other relationships that can be reflected in the total cost of quality include:

- Dollars per share of common stock outstanding
- Dollars as a percent of cost of goods sold
- Dollars as a percent of total manufacturing cost
- Effect of quality leader in its industry.

Why Cost of Quality Programs Fail

"Quality Cost Systems" often have failed to achieve useful results. Major reasons for failure are summarized in Table 4.

Table 4 - Reasons for Failure and Preferred Approach

Reason	Preferred Approach
Accounting Department is ignored because of its lack of cooperation.	Work with accounting to whatever degree it is willing to participate
Quality department insists that certain controversial costs be included.	Agree to exclude or at least separately identify any such costs.
Corporate Quality Department issues one quality procedure without giving each plant the opportunity to review before issuance.	Provide time for plants to comment. Allow enough to care for plant differences.
No provision is made for investing additional funds in prevention activities.	Tell management the amount and type of resource needed to achieve a defined saving.
Role of top management in quality improvement.	Propose numerical goals and identify specific projects. Ask management to provide necessary resources and assign responsibility to the line departments.
No provision is made to obtain the facts needed to diagnose cause of the problems.	Propose some organizational mechanism that will be responsible for diagnoses of causes
Cost data are presented in categories that are too broad to be useful.	Provide detail to the level needed.
System is instituted for all products and departments at one time.	Try it out for one product to obtain a successful case history.
Divisiveness caused by unfair comparisons of results among plants.	Recognize that plants are different. Make comparisons of planned action programs.
Arguments occur about "transfer of charges".	Agree on some arbitrary way to settle the assignment of charges.
Undue emphasis is placed on precision in the figures.	Emphasis should be on identification of problem areas. This does not require extreme precision.
System is personalized. It is associated with an individual who is a strong advocate and sponsor.	Quality cost system should be depersonalized. Tie it in with a structured program of quality improvement that has the support of middle and upper management.
Quality department regards the system as "its own" to maintain.	Turn over data collection and issuance of reports to accounting. Quality Department should concentrate on analysis of the data.

The Initial Cost Study

A common example of how a seemingly innocuous defect is traced through the manufacturing process at a window plant (Lee, 1984). At each point, costs of wasted time and material were calculated. This example illustrated the hidden cost of poor quality and the cost of confusion that results. Table 5 provided the description of events and costs that are associated with poor quality.

Table 5 - Cost of Poor Quality - Window Plant Example

Event	Description	Cost
1	The extrusion department makes 100 pounds of C-800 extrusion that is defective. One flange is bent slightly inward. The defect is not detected. At this point the extrusion has cost $1.16/lb.	$116.00
2	The extrusion moves through several additional processes, including paint. It is stored, handled, and records are kept. The additional cost is $0.19/lb.	$19.00
3	An operator sets up a punch press to notch the ends. The setup requires 0.5 hours @ $11.75/hr.	$5.88
4	An operator attempts to notch the extrusion. The bent flange prevents entry into the punch die. The operator calls for a supervisor and waits 15 minutes. Operator cost is $11.75/hour.	$2.94
5	Supervisor arrives. Operator and supervisor attempt to process the parts without success. They decide to grind out the die so the extrusion with the bent flange will fit into it. All three work to remove the die and take it to the die shop. Total time required is 1.0 hours. Die maker's cost is $13.50/hour.	$40.00

Event	Description	Cost
6	Supervisor, operator, and die maker discuss the problem and attempt to process without success. They decide to grind out the die so the extrusion with the bent flange will fit into it. All three work to remove the die and take it to the die shop. Total time required is 1 hour. The die maker's cost is $13.50/hour.	$40.00
7	Die maker grinds out die, returns to press and sets up the press. Total time is 3.4 hours	$45.90
8	Die maker, operator, and supervisor assemble to determine status. The operation seems to work. Die maker and supervisor go on to other activities, operator prepares to process parts. Total time required is 17.0 minutes.	$11.33
8A	Scheduler spends 1.5 hours @ $15.75/hour to change schedule and advise customers of change.	$23.63
9	Operator processes parts and carries them to the assembly department. Total time for the lot of 100 lbs. of parts is 50 minutes.	$9.79
10	Assembly builds windows with defective parts. Many windows do not operate properly because of the bent flange. Assemblers expend 4.2 extra man hours attempting to make the windows operate. Assembler time costs $10.50/hour.	$44.10
11	An inspector notices that some windows are difficult to operate. She confers with assembler for 15 minutes and decides to summon the inspection supervisor. Inspector's rate is $12.75/hour and inspection supervisor's rate is $17.25/hour.	$5.81
12	The Inspection Supervisor arrives and the Assembly Supervisor comes to see what the problem is. Four persons meet on the problem for 13 minutes and decide to summon the engineer. All wait for an additional 11 minutes until the engineer arrives.	$21.28
13	The engineer, inspection supervisor, assembly supervisor, assembler and inspector confer for 25 minutes and determine a way to fix the problem. All then depart to other activities. The engineer's time costs is $26.75/hour.	$34.27
13A	Inspector documents events - 25 minutes.	$5.31
14	Assembler works for 3.9 hours to repair windows and then sends them to shipping and eventually to the customer.	$40.95

Event	Description	Cost
15	After 2 weeks, customer calls. Some windows worked OK until they were installed. Then the bent flanges caused additional problems. Customer requests a field service engineer to fix the problems. Engineer spends 35 minutes.	$15.60
16	After many phone calls, it is decided to send a field service engineer to the construction site. Times involved in making this decision: Engineer 3.75 hours @ $26.75/hour QA Supervisor 1.75 hours @ $17.25/hour Plant Manager 1.75 hours @ $52.00/hour Field Engineer 1.60 hours @ $17.00/hour	$248.70
17	Field service engineer spends 37 hours in travel to site, fixing problems, and reporting. In addition, engineer spends 1.6 hours on the problem. The sales manager spends 3.4 hours @ $48.00/hour. Travel costs $987.00	$1822.00
18	Weeks later, the same part is run again. It is found that the die can no longer run parts that are in specification because it has been relieved too much. A similar chain of events occurs. The time required: Die Maker 8.0 hours Supervisor 0.5 hours Operator 2.0 hours Engineer 0.7 hours Inspector 0.9 hours	$169.08
	Scrap Value @ $0.17/lb.	($ 17.00)
	Cost of Original Error. . . . .$135.00 Final Cost of Error $2,673.31	

(Lee, 1984)

A study on the cost of poor quality should be made by the organization's cost accountant, but the typical approach followed a different scenario. A quality manager learned about the quality cost concept and discussed the possibility of making a study with the accountant. The accountant's typical response was that "the books are not kept that way." The accountant was able to provide numbers on scrap, rework, or certain other categories, but was not convinced to take the initiative to prepare and define a complete list of categories and collect the data. The quality manager decided that the study should be completed and follows one of two routes:

1. Unilaterally prepare a definition of categories and collect data or

2. Present the limited data provided by the accountant to upper management with a recommendation that a full study be made using the resources of Accounting, Quality, and other functions.

To assure acceptance of the results of the study, the second approach is preferred (Juran, 1979).

A recommended approach is this:

1. Present management with whatever information is readily available to show that the quality problem should be of major concern to the profits of the company. This information has maximum impact if it is in the language of money.

2. Recommend that someone from management should chair a task force to determine costs of poor quality. The task force should include personnel from Accounting and major line functions. The operating committee of the plant can act as the task force, with the study regarded as an agenda item for their meeting

3. Propose a list of categories comprising costs of poor quality. The list can be prepared in a short time by the quality manager using the research on cost of poor quality as well as inputs from the cost and financial accounting departments and other functions.

4. Recommend that upper management finalize definitions and assign responsibilities, with a schedule for data collection, analysis, and presentation of results.

This approach provided an opportunity for upper management to demonstrate leadership on quality, and also assured involvement of relevant departments within the organization so that the study received priority and results were recognized as credible. Without leadership from upper management, the study was likely be made by the Quality manager with minimum input from other department managers. A potential risk was that results may be viewed with skepticism because they were prepared by someone with a biased viewpoint. After categories are developed the next problem is concerned with obtaining the corresponding figures. Two main approaches that have worked in past research:

1. *By estimate*: Using reliable estimates is a practical approach, involving only a modest amount of effort. In a few days or weeks, management and quality managers can determine enough about quality related costs to tell:

   - if there is a major cost reduction opportunity or not, and

   - where this opportunity may be concentrated

2. *By enlarging the accounting system*: This approach is more elaborate, requiring additional cooperative effort from various departments, especially Accounting and Quality. The time to implement this system may require months or years to fully realize its potential.

In the early stages of quality improvement, estimates provide acceptable data. Less work is involved and answers are provided in a shorter time span. The study in Table 5 required approximately three weeks to complete and was conducted in an Industrial Engineering Department by personnel with no prior knowledge of quality costs.

Many companies have chosen to embark on programs of enlarging the accounting system – setting up to compute and publish "quality costs" (Hazlett, 2002). These programs often are delayed due to the time needed to define accounting categories, reach consensus on classifications, set up the data systems, etc. Additional delay has resulted from preoccupation with a level of accuracy that was not needed for managerial decision making.

To illustrate, the cost of defect X in an electronics company was $3 million per year. The figure was an estimate, with actual costs ranging from a low of $2.5 million to a high of $3.5 million. Had the accuracy of the estimates been challenged, managers' response could have been: "All three figures are too high, so let's go after the cost reduction." Over a wide range of estimates, managerial decisions are identical. In the initial study, estimates were within 20% of actual costs and were considered sufficiently accurate for taking managerial action.

The initial study collected cost data from different sources:

1. *Established accounts*: Examples were appraisal activities conducted by an Inspection Department and warranty expenses in response to customer problems.

2. *Analysis of ingredients of established accounts*: For example, an account called "customer returns" could be used to report the cost of

all goods returned. However, returns are made to reduce inventories, as well as to send back defective product. Hence, it may be necessary to go back to the basic return documents to separate the quality costs from normal returns.

3. *Basic accounting documents*: For example, some product inspection is done by Production Department employees. By securing their names and the associated payroll data, it is feasible to quantify these quality costs.

4. *Estimates*: Several approaches may be needed.

   a. *Temporary records*: For example, some production workers spend part of their time repairing defective products. It may be feasible to arrange with their supervisor to create a temporary record to evaluate repair time and thereby the repair cost. This cost can then be extrapolated for the time period to be covered by the study.

   b. *Work sampling*: In another approach, random observations of activities are collected, allowing the percent of time spent in each of a number of predefined categories to be estimated (Salvendy, 1982).

   c. *Allocation*: For example, in an engineering department, some engineers are engaged part time in making product failure analyses. However, the department makes no provision for charging engineering time to multiple accounts. Ask each engineer to estimate time spent on product failure analysis.

d. *Standard costs data*:   Examples include scrap, rework, and replacement of field samples.   Note that such data may be based on obsolete history.

e. *Opinions of knowledgeable personnel*:   Examples are design review, training, etc.

Presentation of Initial Findings to Management

The results can have a striking impact on management if the presentation shows the size of the total cost and identifies areas for improvement. When the report is presented to the appropriate managers, the initiator should be prepared for skepticism and disbelief because of the costs that are associated with poor quality. If management has previously agreed to definitions of the cost categories and if the accounting function has either collected the data or has been a party to the data collection process, the results may be viewed as reliable and valid.

Return on Investment (ROI)

The purpose of quality cost techniques is to provide a tool to management for facilitating quality program and quality improvement activities. Quality cost reports are used to point out the strengths and weaknesses of a quality system. Improvement teams use them to describe the monetary benefits and ramifications of proposed changes. Return-on-investment (ROI) models and other financial analyses can be constructed directly from quality cost data to justify proposals to management. Improvement team members can use this information to rank problems in order of priority. In practice, quality costs define activities of quality program and quality improvement efforts in a language that management can understand and act on-dollars. Any reduction in quality costs have a direct impact on gross profit margins and can be counted on immediately as pretax profit.

Traditional quality cost methods have been around a long time-about a half-century. Through experiences with quality costs over that time, some useful lessons learned include:

1.   The language of money is essential. For a successful quality effort, the single most important element is leadership by upper management. To gain that leadership, we can propose some concepts or tools. That is the wrong approach. Instead, management should be convinced that a problem exists that requires their attention and action (i.e., excessive costs due to poor quality). A quality cost study, particularly when coupled with a successful pilot quality improvement project, is a solid way to gain management support for a broad quality improvement effort. (Excessive cost is one quality-related hot button for management; loss of sales revenue is the other hot button).

2.   Quality cost measurement and publication do not solve quality problems. Managers need to identify improvement projects, establish clear responsibilities, provide resources to diagnose and remove causes of problems, and take other essential steps. New organization machinery is needed to attack and reduce the high costs of poor quality.

3.   The scope of traditional quality costs should be expanded. Traditionally, quality costs have emphasized the cost of nonconformities. Important as this cost is, the need to estimate the cost of inefficient processes. This includes variation

of product characteristics (even on conforming products), redundant operations, sorting inspections, and other forms of nonvalue-added activities. Another area is the cost of lost opportunities for sales revenue.

4.   Traditional categories of quality costs have had a remarkable longevity. About 1945, some pioneers proposed that quality costs be assigned categories of failures, appraisal, and prevention. Many practitioners found the categories useful and even devised ingenious ways to adapt the categories beyond manufacturing (e.g., engineering design) and also to the service sector (e.g., financial services, health care)

Calculating quality's ROI

Once the necessary data are collected, calculating quality return on investment (ROI) is not difficult. In the formula below, "n" equals the amount of money you spent on your quality program during a certain period, and "y" equals the monetary benefit you got in return:

$(y-n)/n * 100 = \%$ ROI

For example, suppose $100,000 was spent last year to implement a new quality program, and $50,000 this year to maintain it. Management decides to track results over the two-year period, so the total investment (n) is $150,000. When the monetary benefits (y) directly related to the quality initiative are tracked over those two years, they amount to $300,000. Applying the ROI formula, the result is:

($300,000 - $150,000)/$150,000 * 100 = 100%

An ROI of 100% means that in two years, the investment was returned, plus a similar amount again as profit. Compared to the 6% or 7% that could be earned from a bank, the quality program was quite a valuable investment!

Gaining Approval for the Quality Improvement Program

Those presenting the results of the cost study should be prepared to answer this question from management: "What action must we take to reduce the cost of poor quality?

The control of quality in many companies has followed a recognizable pattern – as defects increase take action in the form of more inspection. This approach has failed because it usually does not remove the causes of defects (i.e., it is detection but not prevention). To achieve a significant and lasting reduction in costs requires a structured process for attacking the main sources of loss – the failure costs. Such an attack requires proceeding on a project-by-project basis. These projects in turn require resources of various types.

To launch such an attack requires resources, and these must be justified by the expected benefits. Several justifications are possible.

Establish that costs are large enough to justify action (see for example, Table 5).

Use a successful case history (a "bellwether" project) of quality improvement in the company or justify a broader program. Show that opportunities presented by a reasonable goal for cost reduction can be coupled with identification of projects. A typical goal for a structural program on quality improvement is to cut the cost of poor quality in half within 5 years. An important tool in identifying projects is the Pareto analysis which distinguishes between the "vital few" and the "useful many" elements of quality cost. Compare the return on investment from reducing cost of poor quality with the return from investment in added sales. Calculate the improvement in return on investment resulting from improvement in quality. Show the effect of quality improvement on sales income. Although an increase in sales income may be difficult to estimate, it is an intangible factor that can help to justify a quality improvement program. Justification is essential for an effective program of quality improvement.

54

Chapter 3 - Methods

Method

A qualitative research design was used in this study. The case study examined the cost of poor quality that an organization incurs when failing to recognize the importance of implementing procedures to identify all potential failure modes that a product experiences during its manufacturing life cycle. This type of research design is appropriate when using an in-depth examination of a single organization to determine the effects of a phenomenon (cost of poor quality) on profit and return on investment.

Describe the Procedures

A manufacturing organization was used in this study. This organization does not have a method in place to control for poor quality or to track the cost of potential failures to determine their effect on their net profits. A single manufacturing process was described and followed through for this study. Each step of the process was examined, with costs associated with that step detailed. Any potential failures were examined and costs determined if this step of the process experiences failure. At the end of the manufacturing cycle, a cost estimate of both the completed piece and the cost of poor quality was detailed and its effects on the profits of the organization and associated return on investment (ROI).

Data-Gathering Method

Information regarding the cost of poor quality was drawn from cost records on a manufacturing process that has had some quality issues in the past. This information included costs associated with each step of the process, including materials, labor, and overhead. In addition to costs, the researcher spends time observing the manufacturing process to provide a description of each step to characterize the process and determine where breakdowns in the process may occur.

Database of Study

The data that are obtained on the manufacturing process were stored in a data base to allow analysis. A spreadsheet program (i.e., Microsoft Excel) was used to capture the data and determine the costs associated with poor quality.

Validity of the Data

The data included in this study were drawn from corporate records. These costs were used by the company for budget and costs analyses. As a result, the data can be considered valid for the purposes of the present study.

Originality and Limitations of the Data

The data collected on costs are original as they have not been used in research beyond the corporation's internal analysis.

The limitations of the data are that a single process is being examined in this research. As the organization has a myriad of processes at any time, the results of one process may not be generalizable to other processes within the organization.

A second limitation is that the organization in the study may not be representative of other manufacturing organizations. As a result the findings of this study may not be usable by other organizations when planning costs of poor quality analyses, although the research may provide a pattern for their evaluations.

Data Analysis

The data from this study were analyzed using a combination of content analysis of information regarding the manufacturing process that is being studied and financial forecasts that estimate both the costs for manufacturing and the cost of poor quality. These forecasts were used to determine the ROI and effect on gross profit from the process.

Summary

Chapter 3 has presented an overview of the methods that were used in this case study of a single manufacturing process in a large organization. The procedures and data collection processes are described. All data were original and collected from cost records maintained by the organization. In addition, the researcher observed all steps in the manufacturing process to describe the steps and possible areas where breakdowns in quality can occur. The limitations of the study reflect the use of a single process in one organization. The results may not be generalizable beyond this process or organization. The description of the process and associated costs are presented in Chapter 4, with a description of possible manufacturing changes to reduce potential failures included in Chapter 5.

Chapter 4 – Data Results

Data Results

The purpose of this chapter is to present the manufacturing process of a seat belt retractor sensor mechanism that is used to initiate the locking process of a seat belt retractor if the automobile is involved in an accident. The specific steps that are required to complete the assembly and the steps used during this process to assure quality are presented in this chapter, along with costs associated with each step. A problem with quality is included in the process to exemplify costs associated with poor quality and how these costs can affect the profit margin of the corporation. The steps used to correct this problem are also detailed to show how inspections along the assembly process can promote quality, while reducing costs and downtime from poor quality.

The Manufacturing Process

The seat belt retractor sensor mechanism is a part of the seat belt that is assembled separately and then put into the seat belt retractors in vehicles. This part is used to lock the seat belts when the vehicle is involved in an accident or in some cases, when the vehicle stops suddenly or abruptly. A graphic image of this part is presented in Figure 4.

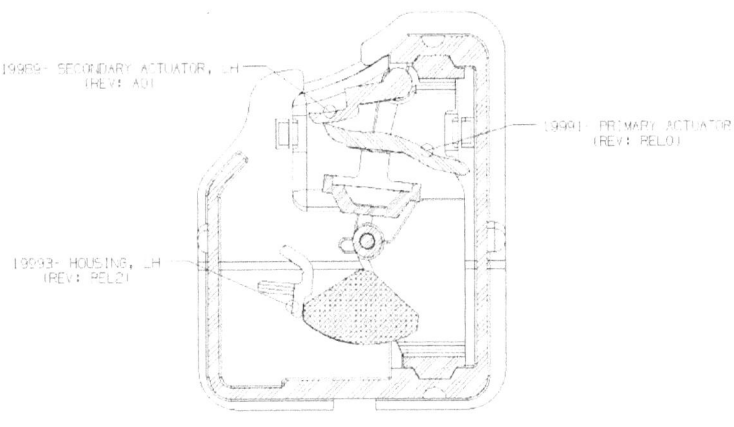

Figure 4 - Seat Belt Retractor Sensor Assembly

This sensor uses two actuators to engage a gear that stops the free spooling of the seat belt webbing. The primary actuator engages the secondary actuator when the swivel assembly changes position within the sensor assembly. This action then prevents the webbing spool from rotating by engaging the gear that is responsible for stopping the webbing spool.

The assembly process has been separated into specific steps that can be quantified. Table 6 presents the steps used to create this assembly.

Table 6 - Seat Belt Retractor Sensor Assembly Process

Step	Process
--	Components are received from the molding department; employees in the assembly area assume that all inspection have been completed on the components and are free from defects.
1	The mass (metal weight) is slid onto the swivel housing by employees
2	Sensor is placed in sensor housing by employees
3	The primary actuator is place on the swivel housing by employees
4	The secondary actuator is attached to the swivel base unit by employees
5	The swivel assembly is attached to the swivel base unit by employees
6	The swivel base unit is attached to the main housing by employees
7	100% of the seat belt retractor sensor units are then tested by employees using automated testing equipment.

The steps included in the assembly process were completed by employees without the help of machines. At each step, the process is open to build variation which can affect the final quality of the individual seat belt retractor sensor units. Each step is completed by a different employee with no inspections for quality completed between operations within the process. As all parts, except the mass (metal weight) and the swivel are plastic, cracks and other defects could be present that could contribute to poor quality and possible product failure. The final inspection process examines 100% of the product after the assembly process is completed, with nonconforming seat belt retractor sensor units sent back for rework.

Costs have been developed for all parts and labor involved in the seat belt retractor sensor assembly process. Table 7 presents the costs associated with building a single seat belt retractor sensor unit.

Table 7 - Seat Belt Retractor Sensor Per Unit Costs

Component Direct Costs	Costs Per Unit
Swivel base unit	$0.03
Main housing	0.03
Swivel housing	0.02
Primary actuator lever	0.02
Swivel mass	0.05
Secondary actuator lever	0.03
Sensor	0.07
Labor (Assemblers)	0.20
Final Inspection/Testing	0.28
Total direct costs	$0.73
Indirect Costs	**Costs per Unit**
Supervision (Line leaders, supervisors, managers)	0.88
Setup	0.23
Maintenance	0.25
Overhead (including profit)	14.91
Total Direct and Indirect Costs	**$17.00**

The total direct cost of the seat belt retractor sensor unit is 73¢. This cost includes both the material costs of each component of the seat belt retractor sensor unit, as well as the direct expenses (labor and inspection/testing) need to assemble the units. In addition, the indirect costs associated with a single unit are $14.91, which includes supervision, setup, and maintenance. The largest cost is overhead which includes the costs associated with the plant (depreciation, insurance, utilities, etc.) and the profit margin that is built into the cost of the unit.

Each finished assembly requires approximately five minutes total labor, with 60 units completed each hour. If at any step in the process, a quality breakdown occurs, the entire assembly process can be halted until the problem is solved. The costs associated with the lack of quality can reduce the company's gross profit as the reimbursement per unit is fixed by contract.

Cost of Poor Quality

When pieces needed for the seat belt retractor sensor were received by the assembly department, no additional quality checks were used to assure that the pieces were free from defects. While these pieces are checked for compliance in the molding department, a random sampling procedure is used and some defects could be missed in this process.

At the first step in the process, the metal weight is slid onto the swivel housing by employees. The metal weights are a purchased item and are assumed to be checked by the manufacturer and are free from defects. The metal weights are casted. After the castings are removed they are cleaned to remove excess metal that squeezes out during the casting process (also known as flashing). If the metal castings have not been cleaned sufficiently, two major defects can result:

1. The excess weight variation could compromise the design intended movement, and

2. The rough edges which could impede movement within the seat belt retractor sensor assembly.

Both of these defects can have a negative affect on the quality of the seat belt retractor sensor assembly process.

This piece is then moved to the second step of the assembly process, which involves placing the sensor in the sensor housing. The sensor is a purchased item that is assumed to be free from defects. The process to make these items requires several steps, with a random inspection of parts both during and after completion of the process. A defect rate of less than 2% of completed sensors is considered adequate for the process. The employee inserting the sensor is relying on the inspection by the manufacturer to assure that the sensor conforms to the seat belt retractor sensor assembly. After inserting the sensor, the assembly is then moved to the next step in the process.

At the third step in the assembly process, the primary actuator is placed on the swivel housing. The primary actuator is molded in house and randomly inspected for defects. The employee at this step in the process is working on a time constraint and assumes that all steps in the process have been completed correctly and the parts used in the process are free from defects.

The secondary actuator is then attached to the swivel base unit in the fourth step of the process. At the sixth step in the process the swivel assembly is attached to the swivel base, with the swivel base attached to the main housing in the seventh step of the process. The same threats that could affect step three are present in steps four, five, and six.

At the completion of the assembly process, the seat belt retractor sensor assemblies are sent for testing. As this assembly is a critical unit in the seat belt assembly, each assembly is checked for performance integrity to the original design intent. The employee responsible for testing the unit places the seat belt retractor sensor assembly in the prescribed orientation and then rotates it through different axes that correlate to positions experienced within normal and adverse vehicle operation (e.g., normal driving, roll-over accident, etc.).

If a failure occurs during the testing process, testing equipment retains the part until an authorized individual (e.g., line leader, supervisor, or manager) retrieves the part, logs the defect, and then reset the testing equipment to clear the error. In logging the defect, the line leader examines the failed part to determine the source of failure and assignable cause of that failure. At this time, the line leader determines if this failure is unique or has been previously noted. If the failure appears to be unique, the seat belt retractor sensor assembly is sent back through the assembly process and reassembled. The part is then retested at an additional cost to the company.

If the failure is part of a pattern of failures, then the line leader may consult with other supervisors and managers to determine the source of the failure (e.g., poorly prepared castings or sensors, molded pieces that have cracks or are short shot that result from lack of adequate plastic materials shot into the molding cavities). The manufacturing staff needs to make decisions on improving the assembly process to assure qualify of the completed parts.

When a pattern of failures is noted, the assembly line has to be halted and the parts needed in the assembly process have to be checked. During this period, the employees are waiting for the inspectors or management staff to complete the audit of materials on hand. If the moldings are found to be deficient, the management staff has to meet with the staff from the molding department to initiate corrective action procedures. If the molding department is in the process of making other parts, they may not have sufficient machine time to run a new batch of molding components to replace the defective units, which can negatively have an effect on production schedules.

During this period, a shortage of moldings for the seat belt retractor sensor assembly may occur, resulting in further downtime by the assembly operators.

If either the weight or sensor is found to be problematic, the supplier quality engineers have to meet with the appropriate suppliers to determine the source and assignable cause of the failure to meet specifications to initiate corrective actions immediately. These actions also could result in a shortage of parts and could result in further downtime for assembly operators.

If the required rate of 60 seat belt retractor sensor assemblies per hour is not met, the seat manufacturer may experience downtime due to a lack of parts. A further domino effect could result at the car assembly plants causing additional shortages in assemblies that include the seat belt retractor sensor assembly.

The costs associated with defects in the assembly process contribute to decreases in the organization's income. If the defects are associated with purchased parts, then the costs attributable to materials can be contained, but labor costs remain. For the molded parts that are created in house, costs associated with poor quality include both materials and labor. Table 8 presents the costs associated with poor quality in the seat belt retractor sensor assembly.

Table 8 - Per Unit Costs Associated with Poor Quality

Component -- Direct Costs	Original Costs	Rework/ Costs of Poor Quality	Total Costs
Molded Parts	.13	.26	.39
Purchased Parts	.12	--	.12
Labor	.20	.40	.60
Final Inspection/Testing	.28	--	--
Re-test Costs	--	.32	.32
Total Direct Costs	.73	1.10	1.83
Indirect Costs			

Supervision (Line Leaders, supervisors, managers)	.88	1.76	2.64
Set up	.23	.69	.99
Maintenance	.25	.00	.25
Overhead (Including Profit)	14.91	--	11.81
Total Direct and Indirect Costs	$17.00	4.65	$17.00

The cost to rework the part includes both materials and labor costs. For example, the purchased parts have no rework costs as the manufacturer has to replace the defective units at no cost to the organization. In contrast, the molded pieces have a rework cost that is double that of the original piece. The costs include remolding the pieces and regrinding the defective pieces. As a result, the costs for the molded parts increased from 13¢ to 39¢ due to the defective materials. Labor also doubles on a per piece basis. The cost to rework the piece, in addition to the cost for the time for the lost unit of production must be considered. For example, if 10 parts are defective, the workers would have to rework the 10 parts and production on new parts would be reduced by 10 units.

The reduction in overhead (including profit) was $3.10 per unit directly reflects on the profitability. As overhead remains constant regardless of the number of units produced, the reduction in the overhead category is a loss to the organization.

Summary

The cost of poor quality is largely hidden, especially in costs associated with production parts that are checked only at the end of the assembly process.

The seat belt retractor sensor is a high volume part that is largely assembled by hand in a multi-step process that can be prone to mistakes. Problems can occur in the parts used in the assembly process prior to beginning assembly. While the small parts are checked randomly for problems, many miscast or mismolded pieces can be missed in the inspection process. The need to maintain production to meet client needs and maintain the profit margin often overrides the need to implement additional quality checks into the assembly process.

Chapter 5 - Summary, Discussion and Recommendations

Summary

Quality has gone from "nice to have" to an imperative in order to compete in business today. As organizations work to maximize profits and improve marketplace position among competitors, an increased emphasis is being placed on quality.

Major quality disconnects (e.g., increasing customer expectations, global competition, and mergers and acquisitions) can affect the ability of companies to sustain sales growth and profitability during times of economic turndown (Beecroft, 1999). One method that can be used to maintain the viability of the organization is through cost cutting. Some organizations respond with a slash-and-burn approach to cost reduction, eliminating productive, as well as nonproductive, activities. To reduce costs effectively, the real business failure costs associated with quality disconnects must be measured. Accurately measuring real (true) failure costs must be systemic and comprehensive. Estimates of "poor quality" costs and expanding accounting systems can be used to generate data into account.

By understanding effects of failure costs on the organization and then implementing actions to minimize causes of these failures can result in cost reductions and improve customer satisfaction with the quality of the products. Customer satisfaction cannot be a frill or a fluke; but must be an imperative for companies wishing to earn or maintain world class stature. Quality is the gateway to American business success in the global free-for-all for customer satisfaction and loyalty.

The fundamental quality cost improvement strategy is to attack failure costs and reduce them to zero. Problem solving and improving processes that produce the product or service are strategies that can be used to accomplish. Optimization of existing quality costs can make significant progress towards cost savings while remaining able to retain talented employees.

Costs for poor quality were not simply the result of factory operation; support operations were also major contributors. The bulk of costs were the result of poor quality. While these costs are often included in the cost accounting standards, they could be avoidable.

Through reduction of costs associated with poor quality, the profit margins could increase and the reputation of the organization in terms of producing a quality product could improve. Many quality specialists implemented vague quality cost "programs" without being clear on the objectives (Juran, 1979) of these programs. Gradually the objectives emerged in two main forms:

1. Estimate the costs of poor quality as a "one-shot" study, and then use the findings to identify specific projects for improvement

2. Expand the accounting system to quantify quality costs, and then publish the results as a continuing scoreboard. The expectation was that the published figures would stimulate managers to take action to reduce the costs.

Expenses associated with quality can be separated into four categories: a) internal failures, b) external failures, c) appraisal costs, and d) prevention costs can track and measure all parameters associated with poor quality. Some of these costs may not be included in typical quality reporting reports. Combining a cost of poor quality and the four costs-of- quality categories together can put the organization in control of the quality system, by shifting from a reaction-based system to one that is proactive in controlling quality.

While incremental costs are important of and by themselves, they do not have the ability to guide management decision making as does total costs. The importance of the grand total is supported by its relationship to other cost categories with which managers are familiar.

When cost summaries on quality are first presented to managers, one typical question is: "What are the right costs?" Managers are looking for a standard ("par") against which to compare their actual costs to help them make an informed judgment on whether there is a need for action. Credible data on the cost of poor quality generally is unavailable, because most companies almost never publish this information. Attempts to conduct research on these costs are ineffective as cost data are confidential and most companies do not release the information. In addition, definitions of quality costs typically vary by company. For example, some companies include unavoidable manufacturing waste as a part of the cost of poor quality while other companies do not. When comparing quality costs for one company with industry averages, three conclusions stand out: a) total costs are higher for complex industries, b) failure costs are the largest percent of the total, and c) prevention costs are a small percent of the total.

Use of the accounting department alone cannot resolve all quality problems in a production process. A more comprehensive method is to include all departmental managers in determining problems associated with quality and present suggestions on developing solutions for these problems to top management to help them understand and recommend appropriate actions.

Detection is not synonymous with solution. Prevention must be the intended result. Results can be assessed by evaluating the overall effects on investment and/or effects on sales and profits. An inverse relationship exists between costs of achieving quality and costs due to lack of quality: as investment in achieving quality increases, costs due to lack of quality decrease.

Setting goals is an important part of controlling costs associated with poor quality. An organization could use a successful case history (a "bellwether" project) of quality improvement in the company to justify implementation of a broader program. Show opportunities presented by establishing reasonable goals for cost reduction coupled with identification of projects. A typical goal for a structural program on quality improvement is to cut the cost of poor quality in half within 5 years.

Methods

The case study research design examined the cost of poor quality that an organization can incur when failing to recognize the importance of implementing procedures to identify all potential failure modes that a product experiences during its manufacturing life cycle. This type of research design is appropriate when using an in-depth examination of a single organization to determine the effects of a phenomenon (cost of poor quality) on profit and return on investment.

Using a single manufacturing process, seat belt retractor sensor assembly, was used in this study. The organization producing this part has one quality process in effect, but this process is at the completion of the assembly process. The present study examined each step of the assembly process, with costs detailed for each step. Any potential failures were examined and costs determined if this step of the process experienced failure. At the end of the manufacturing cycle, a cost estimate of both the completed piece and the cost of poor quality was detailed and its effects on the profits of the organization and associated return on investment (ROI).

Information regarding the cost of poor quality was collected from cost records for the seat belt retractor sensor assembly process that has had some quality issues in the past. This information included costs associated with each step of the process, including materials, labor, and overhead. In addition to costs, the researcher spent time observing the manufacturing process to provide a description of each step to characterize the process and determine where breakdowns in the process could occur.

Data from this study were analyzed using a combination of content analysis of information regarding the assembly process that is being studied and financial forecasts that estimate both costs for manufacturing and the cost of poor quality. These forecasts were used to determine the ROI and its effect on gross profit from the process.

Findings

The process used to manufacture the seat belt retractor sensor assembly combines purchased materials (i.e., mass and sensor) with molded materials created by another department within the organization. In detailing costs associated with each step of the assembly process, total direct costs per unit were 73¢, with indirect costs and overhead (including profit) calculated at $16.27. The organization invoices the seat belt retractor sensor assembly at $17.00 per unit.

The assembly process can be characterized as labor-intensive, error-prone, with each step completed by a different worker. No inspections are completed during the assembly process. However, each seat belt retractor sensor assembly is tested for defects at the end of the process. If a failure occurs, a specific protocol is followed that includes retrieving the part by an authorized individual (e.g., line leader, supervisor, or manager), logging the defect, and resetting the testing equipment. The failed part is inspected by the line leader (or other authorized person) to determine the source of the failure and assignable cause. An evaluation is made to determine if the failure is unique or if the problem is ongoing. If unique, the seat belt retractor sensor assembly is sent back through the system for reassembly. If the problem is systemic, than line leaders consult with other authorized personnel (supervisors or managers) to determine the source of the failure (e.g., poorly prepared castings or sensors, molded pieces that have cracks or are short shot that result from lack of adequate materials shot into the molding cavities). When a pattern of failures is noted, the assembly line must be stopped and parts needed for the process have to be checked. It is at this period, that the workers experience downtime and additional expenses are incurred for inspectors or management staff who have to complete an audit of materials. Each step in the process has a cost. In examining the cost of poor quality for this assembly process, it was determined that a pattern of failures can result in a cost increase that negative effects profits by $3.10 per unit.

Discussion

The cost of poor quality is often unrecognized by upper level managers in a manufacturing organization. In the real-life example of the seat belt retractor sensor assembly, the cost of poor quality could result in a loss in profit of $3.10 per unit. The production standard for this assembly process is 60 units per hour, with two shifts worked in a single day. The plant operates five days a week. Total production is set at 960 per day, 4,800 per week, and 249,600 per year, if peak efficiency is maintained. The potential invoice for these parts $4,243,200. The estimated efficiency is approximately 85%, indicating that 212,160 perfect units should be produced in any given year. The company could invoice these parts at $3,606,720. The difference between total potential production and the estimated efficiency at 85% of total production is $636,480. The effect on profit associated with the loss of

15% of potential production is estimated at $116,064.

If the organization had implemented a program for advanced quality planning using error and mistake proofing methods, potential problems associated with the assembly process could have been recognized while developing the procedures for the assembly process. The management could have established a proactive approach to minimize errors and reduce potential failures. Instead, they react to individual product failures and try to implement corrective action procedures as problems occur.

Recommendations

The company, in recognizing that a problem is occurring in the seat belt retractor sensor assembly process, needs to develop a program to stop errors prior to assembly. They could incorporate a "vision system" that does a 100% inspection of the materials at every step of the process to ensure the integrity of the previous steps in the assembly. A second suggestion that could improve quality is to redesign the assembly process using error and mistake proof techniques and concepts.

The capital costs, estimated at $25,000, associated with these recommendations could be subsidized by the decrease in costs associated with poor quality. The return on investment (ROI) that would be realized is determined by applying the formula $[(y - n) / n] * 100$, where y is the monetary benefits resulting from implementing the quality program and n is the amount of money spent on the quality program. The ROI realized by this quality program is 364.25, which indicates that implementing this type of program could substantially improve the net profit of the organization.

While the present study used a single assembly process to illustrate the costs associated with poor quality and the effects obtained from implementing corrective actions to prevent product failure. Further research is needed to determine if the corrective action has had the anticipated effects. Additional research is needed to examine other assembly processes to determine where product failures are occurring and if these failures can be minimized during the manufacturing process.

Bibliography

Beecroft, D. (1999). *Quality Costs: Application in non-manufacturing organizations*. Paper presented at the Annual Quality Congress Proceedings, Milwaukee.

Chase, N. (1999). Cost of Quality. *Baldridgeplus* (January), 777.

Creveling, C. M. (2000). *Engineering Methods for Robust Design*: Addison Wesley.

Gryna. (1988). An Emerging Cost of Quality Model. *Japanesse Union of Scientist and Engineers*, 13.

Houston, D. (2001). Cost of Software Quality. In J. B. Keats (Ed.), *A Means of Promoting Software Process Improvement* (pp. 13).

Juran, J. M. (1979). *Quality Control Handbook* (Third Edition ed.): McGraw Hill.

Knackstedt, T. (2003). *Quality Terminology Explained*. Retrieved 03/11/03, 2003, from http://www.kwaliteg.co.za/glossary.htm

Lee, Q. (1984). The Cost of Quality. *Strategos*, 4.

Lindland, W. a. (1996, 1996). Paper presented at the Optimized Quality for a Lean Industry, Chicago, Ill.

Quartararo, A. (1999, 11/08/99). The Cost of Quality in Enterprise GIS. *Directions Magazine*.

Ragsdell, D. K. (2001). Introduction to Robust Engineering. On *Supplier Workshop*. Rolla.

Salvendy (Ed.). (1982). *Process Control for Manufacturing*.

www.ingramcontent.com/pod-product-compliance
Lightning Source LLC
Chambersburg PA
CBHW070133210526
45170CB00013B/860